# The Japanese Canadians

**Multicultural Canada Series**
**Series Consultant: Daniel Hill**

# The Japanese Canadians

## Roy Ito

 **Van Nostrand Reinhold Ltd., Toronto**
**New York, Cincinnati, London, Melbourne**

Library of Congress Number 77-89871

Canadian Cataloguing in Publication Data

Ito, Roy, 1922-
  The Japanese Canadians

(Multicultural Canada series)

ISBN 0-442-29891-9 pa.

1. Japanese in British Columbia – Juvenile literature.
I. Title. II. Series.

FC3850.J3186    j971.1′004′956    C77-001476-3
F1089.7.J3186

**Acknowledgements**
The following sources of illustration are acknowledged: British Columbia Provincial Archives, 19; Canadian Broadcasting Corporation, 61 (top left); Susan Hidaka, 64; Roy Ito, 9, 12, 53, 55; Japanese Canadian Cultural Centre, 6, 15, 18, 21, 26, 36, 37, 41, 43 (both); 45, 50, 51, 52 (left), 57 (top right); Sam Kayama, 32; Mrs. W. Kuwabara, 23; Raymond Moriyama, 60 (right); Harry Naganobu, 11; National Film Board, 61 (top left); Paterson Photographic Works, 16, 49, 56 (both), 58, 59 (all), 63 (both); Public Archives of Canada, 25 (PA 931), 52 (right) (C24452); Tom Shoyama, 61 (top right); Ron Tamaki, 57 (lower left, top right); George Tanaka, 60 (top left); United Church Archives, 28, 29, 38 (top right), 38-39; University of British Columbia, Special Collection, 8, 27; Vancouver Public Library, 7, 13, 31, 47, 48; Tom Yoshida, 44. Japanese characters on pages 34 and 35 by Katsu Morino. Information for the maps was supplied by: Sam Kayama, 39; Harry Naganobu, 42.

The author wishes to acknowledge the assistance given by the Japanese Canadian Citizens' Association with the translation of certain material published in Japanese. Special thanks are due to the staff of the Japanese Canadian Cultural Centre in Toronto.

Editorial director: Garry Lovatt
Design: Peggy Heath
Production supervisor: Beth Potter
Cover photography: Paterson Photographic Works
Maps and diagrams: Julian Cleva
Typesetting: Fleet Typographers Ltd.
Printing and binding: Ashton-Potter Ltd.
Film: John Downey & Son Ltd.
Printed and bound in Canada
    81 82 83    8 7 6 5 4

# Contents

# The First Japanese Immigrants

It was not until 1884 that the Japanese government permitted its people to emigrate to North America. A few years before, in 1877, the first Japanese man somehow came to Canada from the United States. His name was Manzo Nagano. Nagano went to work fishing for salmon on the Fraser River with an Italian. Later he worked on the docks in Vancouver – it was called Gastown then – before returning to Japan. He came back to Canada in 1892 and settled in Victoria, where he opened a store on Government Street.

Another early Japanese pioneer was Mr. Takizo, who arrived soon after Manzo Nagano. We do not know his first name. His friends called him Takiji-san. Takiji-san had worked as a sailor on a ship that hunted sea otter off the British Columbia coast. When he came to Vancouver, he found work at Hastings Mill. Machines at this sawmill cut up the huge trees that covered the land where the city of Vancouver now stands.

Takiji-san could speak a little English and got along well with the white people. He opened a boarding house for the earliest Japanese immigrants. They were men who had worked mostly on sealing ships. Takiji-san obtained jobs for them at Hastings Mill. The men worked hard and the company hired more Japanese. Nearly all Japanese coming to Canada in those days seemed to find work at Hastings Mill. They were very loyal to the company, calling it the Helping Hand Company, because it helped them get started in the new country.

Many of these immigrants felt very alone and homesick. Most lived in very crude shacks, worked long hours, and did not have many pleasures. They missed Japan and their families. The first Japanese woman to come was Mrs. Washiji Oya in 1887, who joined her husband. Few other women followed at that time.

Since most could not speak English, communicating with the white people was often difficult. Sometimes unfortunate

*Mrs. Washiji Oya, the first Japanese woman to settle in Canada.*

Right: *Loading lumber on sailing ships docked at Hastings Mill wharf, Vancouver. The photograph was taken at the end of the nineteenth century.*

1. To make yourself understood to other people when you do not understand their language can be very difficult.
   a. Act out the story of Ishikawa, Yamada and the foreman.
   b. Pretend that you cannot speak English and have something to tell members of your group. The group should try to understand what you want to say.
2. Make a list of the 25 words in the English language that your group thinks would be most useful to a non-English-speaking immigrant who has just arrived in Canada. Compare your list with those made by other groups.
3. *Basic English* is a selected vocabulary of 850 English words. It has been used to teach immigrants to communicate in English. Find information about Basic English in an encyclopedia. Try to write the story of "The First Japanese Immigrants" in Basic English.

misunderstandings arose. In 1892 Suteya Yamada and Katsuzo Ishikawa were working together at Hastings Mill. Their job was to pile railway ties, which were very heavy and awkward. Ishikawa accidentally hit Yamada, and the pain was so great that Yamada had to sit down. The foreman came along. He thought Yamada was sitting down on the job and fired him. Yamada could not explain. Many days later after a great deal of effort he got his job back.

In the spring of the following year Yamada was working on a machine. A piece of metal broke loose and struck him on the head. Remembering what had happened before, he did not leave his machine. Wiping away the blood from his wound, he kept on working. The foreman ordered Yamada to get first aid, but he did not understand and kept working. The foreman tried to pull him away. Yamada refused and clung to the machine. At last another Japanese who understood a little English came along and explained everything to Yamada. Although still in pain, Yamada returned to work next day. He wished he understood English.

Right: *Felling a Douglas fir. Three Japanese Canadians pose beside the giant tree they are cutting. The man on the left holds a two-man saw. Many Japanese found work in logging and lumbering.*

# The Buddhist Churches of Canada

The first Buddhist minister came to Canada from Japan in 1904 to serve the Japanese immigrants. Today there are 16 Buddhist churches in Canada. Most of the 5000 members are Japanese Canadians.

Most churches meet once a week, usually on Sundays, for worship. Services are conducted in English and Japanese. In the Sunday schools children learn that Buddha teaches:

I shall not harm living things.
I shall not take what does not belong to me.
I shall not do anything impure.
I shall not tell falsehoods.
I shall not take harmful food and drinks.

In a Buddhist church the figure of Buddha occupies the central portion of the altar. In some churches a scroll may be hung in place of the figure. The scroll has Japanese writing that reads "I place my faith in Buddha."

Flowers, candies, rice and fruits are offered in praise and thanksgiving for Buddha's guidance. Incense is offered to symbolize the act of purifying one's mind.

Buddhist churches have groups for boys and girls, young married couples and older people. Some of them have classes in *ikebana*, or flower arrangement, and Japanese folk dancing. The groups take an interest in community activities and problems.

When a Buddhist dies, he is given a Buddhist name which is called a *ho-myo*. An evening service, the *otsuya*, is held by relatives before the day of the funeral.

Japanese Buddhists believe that the dead do not go right away to the other world. Additional services are usually held on the seventh and the forty-ninth days. Services are also held on the first, second, sixth and twelfth anniversaries. The people pray for the happiness of the dead in the other world.

*Altar of a Buddhist church in Canada.*

9

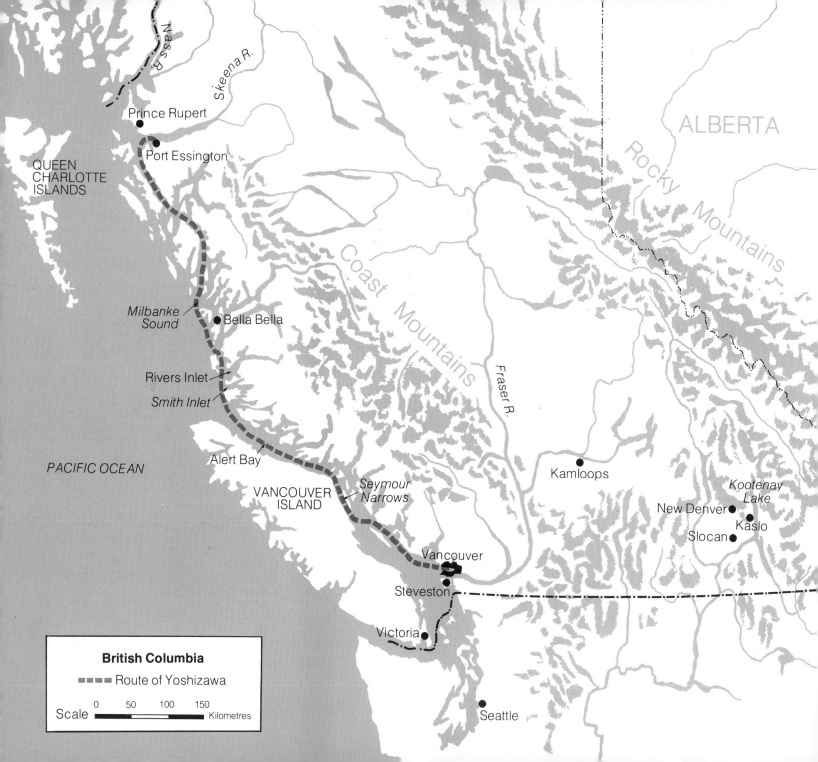

Nass R.

Skeena R.

Prince Rupert

Port Essington

QUEEN
CHARLOTTE
ISLANDS

ALBERTA

Rocky Mountains

Coast Mountains

*Milbanke
Sound*

Bella Bella

Rivers Inlet

*Smith Inlet*

PACIFIC OCEAN

Alert Bay

VANCOUVER
ISLAND

*Seymour
Narrows*

*Fraser R.*

Kamloops

*Kootenay
Lake*

New Denver

Kaslo

Slocan

Vancouver

Steveston

Victoria

Seattle

### British Columbia

▬▬▬ Route of Yoshizawa

Scale  0   50   100   150

Kilometres

1. Use the scale on the map of British Columbia to find which of the following figures is closest to the distance Yoshizawa and his men rowed: 350 km; 600 km; 800 km; 1000 km.
2. How long did it take them to make this journey?

## SEEKING WORK ON THE SKEENA

By 1890 one hundred Japanese worked at Hastings Mill and 2000 fished for salmon on the Fraser River. One young man, Yasukichi Yoshizawa, who worked at Hastings Mill worried about this. He wondered where new Japanese immigrants were going to find work. Everyone could not work at Hastings Mill or go fishing on the Fraser.

He heard that there was a great salmon river called the Skeena to the north. Why not go north and find work? He talked over his idea with a friend, Shiga Aikawa, and they persuaded three other men to go with them. The five men bought a rowboat, a gun, a fishing line, a map of the coast, four bags of flour, a bag of potatoes, a small can of baking powder, and a bottle of *shoyu* – Japanese soy sauce. On Friday, April 8, 1890, they left Vancouver.

Things did not go well at first. Yoshizawa found that he was the only one who could row. He couldn't imagine a Japanese not being able to row since all of Japan is close to the sea. Yoshizawa and Aikawa were the only ones who had rubber clothing and footwear. This was a real hardship since there were many rainy days. They had a difficult time rowing through the Seymour Narrows where the waters speed up to fifteen knots and hidden rocks have wrecked many ships. It was only possible to go through during slack tide. They had to wake at five o'clock one morning to pass through the Narrows.

Yoshizawa thought the trip would take 20 days. On the twentieth day they were at Smith Inlet, which was only half way. When food ran out they fished, hunted, and traded with Indians. Daily they pulled on the oars. It was the forty-second day before Point Lambert near the mouth of the Skeena River came into sight.

The sound of hammering and sawing echoed over the water. One hundred men were hard at work building the North Pacific Cannery. The white people and the Indians were startled when Yoshizawa and his men landed. They had never seen a Japanese before. They were even more surprised when they learned they had rowed all the way from Vancouver.

*Yasukichi Yoshizawa rowed with four other men from Vancouver to the Skeena River in 1890.*

1. Imagine you and four companions are going to retrace Yoshizawa's voyage in a rowboat. Make a list of the items you would take. Compare your list with the list of Yoshizawa's supplies.
2. Imagine you made a trip similar to Yoshizawa's. Write a letter to a friend describing the last two weeks of the trip.

Below: *The coast of British Columbia.*

The five Japanese started work cutting firewood for winter. With poor tools they could only cut enough to buy food. They were living in a tent. Three of the men became very discouraged. They heard that there were plenty of jobs in Seattle where many men were working, rebuilding the city after a great fire. All three decided to go back to the south. The gun was sold to pay for their boat fare.

When the fishing season began, Yoshizawa partnered with a white man and Aikawa with an Indian. They began to fish for salmon on the Skeena River. Four years later some 80 Japanese were fishing on the Skeena. They came because Yoshizawa and Aikawa proved to be good fishermen, and the cannery owners wanted more Japanese fishermen.

Opposite page: *Immigrants aboard S.S.* Kumeric, *about 1907, in Vancouver Harbour. Japanese, Chinese, and Sikhs from India were on the ship. Members of all three groups are visible in this photograph. Can you identify them?*

# The First Generation:
# Mankichi and Oya Omura

## ARRIVAL OF MANKICHI OMURA

In Japan in the province of Fukuoka-ken Mankichi Omura worked hard in his father's field. It was 1908 and Mankichi was seventeen years old. As he worked he thought about the stories he had heard the night before. A Japanese who had just come back from Canada spoke about the wonders of a place called British Columbia. Salmon by the thousands came swarming into the river mouths; giant trees were chopped down to make lumber; there was plenty of land. Everyone had a chance to make money.

Mankichi thought of his prospects in Japan. It was difficult to make a comfortable living. Why not go to Canada, get a good job and return to Japan within five years with plenty of money? He decided to borrow money for his fare.

Before he left the village his parents and friends gave him a party. They urged him to eat plenty of Japanese food, saying, "You won't get these in Canada." Each wished him well, and expected him back soon as a rich man. *"Hayaku kokyo ni nishiki kazare,"* they said, which meant "Come back as soon as possible in your golden clothes."

After a long voyage of eighteen days the ship docked in Vancouver. It was September 1908. Mankichi paid the entry fee of $25 and landed in Canada. All his belongings were in his *yanagi kori,* a small wicker basket. He was met by people from Fukuoka-ken, his home province. They found him a place to stay on Powell Street, where many Japanese lived and owned stores. A man who came from the same village found him a job at Hastings Mill. Soon Mankichi was piling lumber and earning $1.30 per day. It was hard work but he didn't mind.

He lived in a small room in a rooming house on Powell Street. The food was simple but plentiful, and it was all cooked in the Japanese way. He didn't spend money foolishly as his aim was to save. In his spare time he liked to watch a Japanese baseball team or go fishing in Burrard Inlet. Sometimes he walked to Stanley Park. But it was a lonely life.

Mankichi wanted to learn English and after a hard day's work he went to the Japanese Mission of the Methodist Church. Often he was too tired to stay awake, but he learned enough from the patient teachers to talk a little English.

Right: *A group of young Japanese Canadians in Vancouver photographed outside a rooming house on Powell Street about 1910.*

*In Japan you eat with your eyes.*

HIGHLIGHT

# Japanese Food

The basic Japanese food is boiled rice. The rice is washed thoroughly and drained. For every 185 g of rice grains 360 mL of water is added. It is left for one hour in a covered pot before cooking. The cooked rice should not be too hard or too soft. As soon as vapour starts to escape from the pot the heat is turned down. An experienced cook can tell from the smell of the steam when the rice is done.

On special occasions such as weddings rice is steamed with red beans. This dish is called *sekihan*. Boiled rice is also used to make *sushi*, a rice cake that can be served with any kind of meat, fish or vegetable. *Gomoku meshi* is white rice with cooked vegetables and meat. *Nigiri meshi*, or rice balls, are often prepared for picnics.

*Shoyu* or soy sauce is used like salt in Japanese cooking to flavour meat, fish and vegetables. It gives the food its particular taste and smell.

**CHICKEN RICE,**
**a recipe you can try.**

**Ingredients**
650 g uncooked rice
1 L chicken soup
450 g of cooked chicken meat
50 mL soy sauce

*Slice* the chicken and soak in the soy sauce for 15 minutes. Remove the chicken from the soy sauce.
*Mix* the soy sauce into the chicken soup.
*Wash* the rice thoroughly three times.
*Add* the chicken soup to the rice and cook in a closed container. When steam starts to escape, turn the heat to low for 15 minutes. Turn the heat to simmer another 10 minutes.
*Turn* the heat off and wait 15 minutes before serving, placing the sliced chicken on top of the rice.

## Using Chopsticks

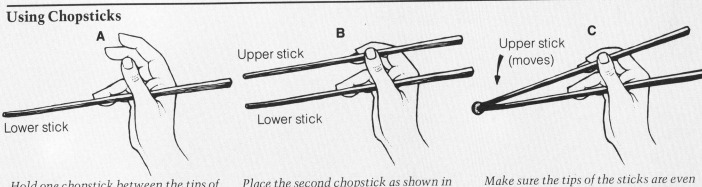

Hold one chopstick between the tips of the fourth and little fingers. This chopstick remains firm in this position as you eat (A).

Place the second chopstick as shown in B. Hold this upper stick with the thumb, index and middle finger as you would a pencil. There should be about 3 cm between the sticks.

Make sure the tips of the sticks are even by tapping them gently on the table. Now use the middle and index fingers to move the upper stick towards the lower stick. Pick up the food (C).

Mankichi earned good money compared to wages in Japan, but he could see he wouldn't become a rich man quickly. Most of the Japanese worked in sawmills, in mines, and on the railway. Others had small farms. Mankichi heard that in fishing it was possible to earn a large sum in a good year. He spoke to the people of the Fukuoka-ken Society and it was arranged that he would go to the Skeena River to become a fisherman.

## Ken Societies

The Japanese community in Vancouver had many *ken* societies. Immigrants from each province or *ken* in Japan set up a "helping-hand" society to aid people from their area. Mankichi and later his son, Kenji, belonged to the Fukuoka-ken Society, because Mankichi came from Fukuoka-ken. Two or three times a year the people of the society got together for picnics and meetings. In times of difficulty, Kenji knew that the Fukuoka-ken Society would help him.

Left: *A Japanese Canadian family in the Fraser Valley. Many of the farmers took up small-fruit farming.*

Right: *Two Japanese Canadians at work in a barrel factory. Eighty years ago, wooden barrels were widely used for packaging.*

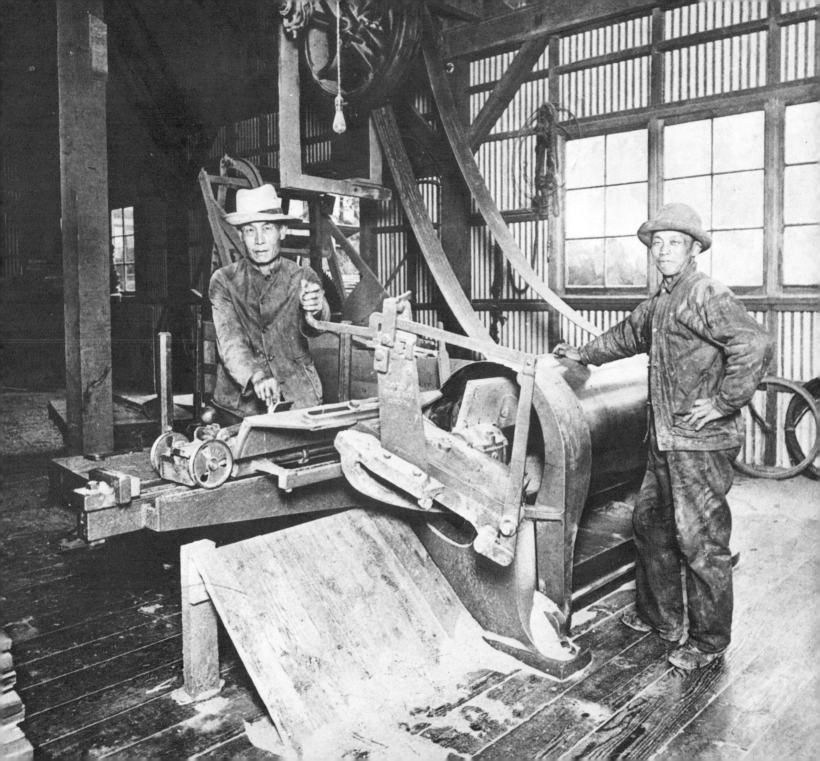

In 1908 when Mankichi arrived, most of the Japanese Canadians lived in the Vancouver area. Large numbers of women first came in 1908. With their arrival, homes were started and family life began.

### Emigrants from Japan by Destination, 1885-1907

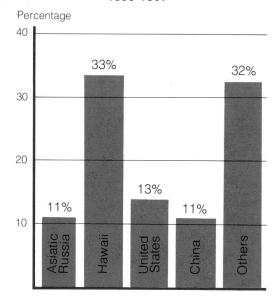

Percentage

### Emigrants from Japan by Destination, 1885-1924

| Destination | 1885-1907 | 1908-1924 | 1885-1924 | % |
|---|---|---|---|---|
| Asiatic Russia | 59 273 | 243 673 | 302 946 | 25.6 |
| Hawaii | 178 927 | 59 831 | 238 758 | 20.2 |
| United States | 72 545 | 123 998 | 196 543 | 16.6 |
| China | 58 388 | 46 870 | 105 258 | 8.9 |
| Canada | 10 513 | 19 278 | 29 791 | 2.5 |
| Brazil | 34 | 25 913 | 25 947 | 2.2 |
| Philippines | 2 175 | 19 148 | 21 323 | 1.8 |
| Peru | 1 108 | 19 876 | 20 984 | 1.8 |
| Korea | 72 027 | — | 72 027 | 6.1 |
| Australia | 7 540 | — | 7 540 | 0.6 |
| Other countries | 77 161 | 84 667 | 161 828 | 13.7 |
| Total | 539 691 | 643 254 | 1 182 945 | 100.0 |

1. The table shows where emigrants from Japan were going from 1885-1924. Which three areas received most Japanese from 1885-1907? from 1908-1924? and from 1885-1924?
2. How many Japanese migrated to another land up to 1924?
3. What percentage of these went to Canada?
4. Look up the meaning of *immigrant* and *emigrant*. What is the difference?
5. The bar graph shows some of the information given in the table.
   a. Look up the latest Canada Year Book and find out which ten countries sent the greatest number of people to Canada during the last ten years.
   b. Using the bar graph (left) as a guide, present your findings in the form of a bar graph.
6. Interview some immigrants in your neighbourhood to find out why they came to Canada. Make a summary of the results. Include the number of immigrants surveyed. Try to group the answers you receive – for example, how many came to Canada hoping to improve their standard of living? How many came to visit and then stayed?

# FISHING ON THE SKEENA

Towed by a gas-engine powered boat, the line of fishing skiffs headed downstream toward the mouth of the Skeena River. Mankichi sat in one of the leading boats. He was the helper of Matasaburo Yonemura, who had been fishing on the Skeena out of Port Essington for 12 years.

As they neared the fishing area, the skiffs broke away from the towboat. The men rowed to what they hoped was a good location. The river was now filled with white, Indian, and Japanese fishermen watching for the signal that would begin the fishing week. Promptly at 6 P.M. the gun boomed.

Yonemura threw the wooden buoy with a flag marker into the river. Then he pushed the gill net into the river while Mankichi rowed steadily. Mankichi kept his eyes on the buoy and the cork line to make sure he was rowing in a straight line. When the 400-metre net was safely in, they sat down to watch. It was not long before Yonemura pointed to a bobbing cork. "A sockeye," he said. There was a splash further down the line; a fish was caught near the surface. A cork disappeared completely. "A spring salmon," Yonemura said.

They unhitched the net and rowed to the place where the cork had vanished. Yonemura leaned over and slowly pulled up the mesh. The gaffing hook was ready in his right hand. He gently lowered the hook and triumphantly brought up a huge fish. It was silver blue, and over a metre long. Yonemura made a small cut in the tail. The flesh was red. A red spring salmon was worth five times more than a white spring salmon.

After three hours of drifting with the tide, they brought in their net, Mankichi hauling it in, and Yonemura working the oars. They had caught 26 sockeye, three springs, and one small jack salmon. It was a good start to the season.

They worked hard all summer. Yonemura taught Mankichi all he knew about boat-handling, river currents, tides, and fishing. Day and night they put out the net, sleeping when they could. Their boat had no shelter except for a small tent. On rainy days they were cold and wet. Other days the water was rough and the work harder.

*Fishing boats on the west coast early in the twentieth century. These gill-netters carried sails, and were called Columbia River boats.*

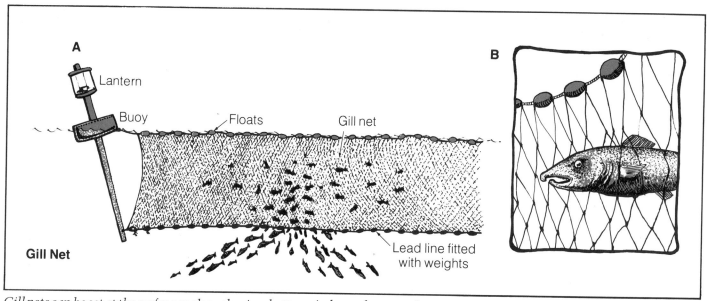

*Gill nets can be set at the surface or along the river bottom. A shows the net at the surface. B illustrates a fish trapped by its gills in the net.*

The collector boat from the canning company came around once a day to take the fish. They learned the latest news from the crew. Yonemura, usually a man of few words, became quite angry when he talked of how Japanese fishermen were treated. Other fishermen were free to move from the Skeena to the Nass River, or to Rivers Inlet, or to the Fraser. Not so the Japanese. Their licences kept them in one area. There was nothing they could do about it, as the Japanese in British Columbia were not allowed to vote. Yonemura intended to make Canada his home and get the vote.

At the end of the fishing season, Mankichi returned to Vancouver to the rooming house on Powell Street. His summer earnings came to $325. Each summer he went north to the Skeena and fished. Each fall he returned to Vancouver. For two years he partnered with Yonemura, and in the third year he obtained his own licence. He rented a boat and a net from the cannery and went to work for himself.

1. Use a reference to find the names of the different kinds of Pacific salmon. For each, note the size and appearance.
2. Find information on the life cycle of the sockeye salmon. Prepare a chart to show the cycle.
3. On the British Columbia coast, three methods are used to catch salmon – gillnetting, purse seining, and trolling. Find information about these methods and make a report using diagrams.

## SOME HAD JAPANESE NAMES

*Sergeant Masumi Mitsui was in the 10th Battalion. He was awarded the Military Medal for bravery at the Battle of Hill 70 in 1917. Mr. Mitsui now lives in Hamilton, Ontario.*

In December, 1915, Mankichi saw an item in the Japanese language newspaper. War had broken out in Europe earlier in 1914, and Canada had followed Britain into the conflict. The Canadian Japanese Association was asking for volunteers to serve in the Canadian Army. By fighting for their new country, Japanese immigrants could show that they were Canadians. Mankichi thought about this. He knew now that he would not be going back to Japan as a rich man. His future was in Canada. As a Canadian he had to carry out his responsibilities. Mankichi decided to volunteer.

Mankichi and 200 Japanese volunteers paraded on Powell Street baseball grounds under the watchful eye of a sergeant major. All expenses were paid by the Japanese community. The Canadian Japanese Association wired Ottawa that the volunteers were ready. When the reply came Mankichi found it difficult to understand. It said that there was no place in the Canadian Army for the Japanese. The white people claimed that the Japanese would never assimilate with other Canadians. They said the Japanese had peculiar customs, a strange language, and a different appearance, and that they would never make good Canadian citizens. The volunteers were disbanded. Mankichi went back to the Skeena for another fishing season.

He was painting his boat when he heard the blast of a ship's whistle. It was the Union Steamship Company boat from Vancouver on its way to Prince Rupert. He went down to the cannery dock to watch the passengers land. One of the volunteers from Vancouver came running down the gangplank in a Canadian Army uniform. With him was a young officer.

"Oi!" he yelled at Mankichi. "We can get in. Come on! Pack your things and let's go!"

The volunteer had answered the call for men to enlist in Alberta. The recruiting officer there had learned from him that other Japanese were prepared to join the army. He had been sent with an officer to recruit as many of the volunteers as he could find to enlist in Alberta.

## The Canadian Japanese Association

The Canadian Japanese Association was organized in 1900 by business and professional people. It tried to speak for the community. It was originally formed to give support to Mr. Tomekichi (Tomey) Honma, who tried to win the right to vote for the Japanese. (In 1895 all Asians were excluded from the vote in British Columbia.) He took his case to court, but was not successful in gaining the vote.

In 1977 a new $4 million school (Tomey Honma Junior Secondary School) was named after him in Steveston, British Columbia. The school board said, "It is an honour to have the school named after Tomey Honma, who fought for human rights and democracy."

Opposite page: *Wounded Canadian soldiers, including a Japanese Canadian, at a casualty clearing station during World War I. The men brought the dog out of the trenches with them, and presented it to the nurse.*

With 56 Japanese volunteers, all from British Columbia, Mankichi enlisted in the 175th Overseas Battalion in Medicine Hat, Alberta. After training they left for Europe on September 6, 1916. From the Seaford Army Base in England the Japanese soldiers were sent to France to join the 50th Battalion of the Canadian Fourth Division.

The Canadian Army spent the winter of 1916 to 1917 getting ready to attack Vimy Ridge. This was a low height of land, about 11 kilometres long. The French had already tried to capture the Ridge with the loss of a great many men. One day the Battalion formed a square and a senior officer spoke to the men. He told them that they would be going into battle soon. For the first time, Canadians would fight as an army. The volunteers, he said, all represented Canada. The Japanese heard this with pride. They were called Canadians for the first time.

On Easter Monday, April 9, 1917, at 5.30 A.M. a thousand guns began firing on enemy positions on Vimy Ridge. Mankichi, hugging the slope, saw the flashes from the gun lines behind him and heard the shells passing overhead. Machine guns clattered. A wet snow blew from the north-west. He heard the bagpipes playing.

The first group started to cross no-man's land. The 50th and 44th Battalions of the 10th Brigade were held back, as they were to attack a slight rise known as the Pimple. But next day the two battalions were ordered to move toward Hill 145. The Hill was strongly defended, and many Canadians had been killed. Reinforcements were needed. The two battalions were called on to help.

The big guns began to land shells on the Hill. Mankichi charged up the slope with the others. There was a great deal of shouting and firing of guns. Men began to fall. Using their bayonets, the Canadians finally captured Hill 145.

For two days the men of the battalion rested. The Pimple had still to be captured. In a blinding snowstorm, Mankichi and the men of the 50th and other battalions fought. Two hours after the attack had begun, the Pimple was taken. The 50th Battalion lost many men. Hill 145 and the Pimple were two of the hardest battles fought on Vimy Ridge.

The capture of Vimy Ridge was called Canada's greatest victory. The newspapers said that April 9 was the day Canada became a nation. Ten thousand Canadians were wounded, 3600 were killed. They represented all the different groups in Canada. Some had Japanese names.

By the end of the war, of the 56 Japanese in the 50th Battalion, 20 were killed and 23 wounded. Others were killed and wounded serving with the 10th and 52nd Battalions. The men who died had names like Yamasaki, Tada, Ishii, Takeuchi, Hamaguchi, Hayashi, Inouye, Nakamura, Ban, Harada, Ishihara, Tsuchiya, Katayama, Takahashi, Yomiya, Moro-oka....

# PICTURE BRIDE

Mankichi Omura returned from service in the army in 1919, and settled down in Port Essington. He rented a house next door to Yonemura. It was eleven years since he had left his parents' home in Fukuoka-ken.

Mankichi needed a wife. He did not have the money to go back to Japan himself, so he asked his parents to find him a bride. They chose a young woman, named Oya, from a good, hard-working family. Oya's parents sent her photograph to Mankichi. He studied it carefully. She seemed satisfactory.

Mankichi borrowed a camera and Yonemura took a picture of him in his work clothes in front of his boat. He didn't want Oya to get wrong ideas. Some men sent pictures taken when they were much younger, or in borrowed clothes. He mailed Oya the picture and a letter asking her to marry him. Oya agreed, and with both sets of parents visited the village registry office. The marriage was noted in the *Koseki*, the village records.

The ship Oya sailed on docked at Vancouver in spring, 1920, after a two-week voyage. She was very tired and bewildered. On the ship she had eaten strange food with metal utensils. She thought the white people were terribly big. Now she would have to wear western clothes for the first time. Mankichi tried to be kind and thoughtful. He took her to his friends who owned the rooming house on Powell Street. From there they were married in a Buddhist church.

Left: *The Japanese Canadian war memorial in Stanley Park, Vancouver. It is inscribed with the names of the 54 Japanese Canadians killed in World War I.*

Right: *A picture bride, about 1915. This couple were more prosperous than most of the Japanese immigrants. The bride is dressed in the traditional costume.*

## Haiku

When life in the trenches was too boring, some of the Japanese soldiers wrote *haiku*. A haiku is a short poem of three lines. There are five syllables in the first line, seven syllables in the second line, and five syllables in the third line. Haiku are usually about nature and they often refer to the seasons.

These haiku were translated from verse written by Japanese poets.

> The perfectly still
> earth, with eyes almost closed
> enters into winter.

> Like a diamond
> a drop of dew, all alone
> on a cold, cold stone.

Try writing a haiku.

1. Make a list of difficulties that Oya may have faced when she came to Canada.
2. Interview married couples who have come to Canada to find out if one of the pair had more problems than the other adjusting to the new life. Can you draw any conclusions from these findings?

*Unloading a collector boat at a cannery wharf.*

On the ship going to Port Essington, Mankichi told Oya how Yoshizawa and Aikawa had rowed from Vancouver to the Skeena. He spoke to her of Yonemura and the life of a salmon fisherman. He described Port Essington and their house. It had three rooms, and a kitchen with a wood stove and running water. There was no electricity but there were bright kerosene lamps. He had bought her a sewing machine, and they had good strong furniture.

When the ship reached Port Essington, Yonemura and their other neighbours were at the cannery wharf to welcome Oya Omura to her new home in Canada.

## FISHING LICENCES

With the money from his army service Mankichi bought a boat and a net. Now he was a full-time fisherman. In April he fished for spring salmon. The sockeye season started in July, and the fishing community bustled with men from the south. At the end of August, it was the cohoe season, and the summer men returned to their homes in Vancouver. Mankichi fished into the cold days of October. Then he hauled in his boat and net, and spent the winter repairing his equipment. He cut firewood to keep their house warm. In his spare time he caught up on his sleep, and read Japanese newspapers and magazines. It was a good life.

But there were moments when he talked to Yonemura that made him uneasy. When, Yonemura often asked, would the Japanese be allowed to vote? Even the veterans of the war did not have this right. They were going to need some kind of voice, because the white people were saying that there were too many Japanese fishermen. A government commission had been set up to look into the question of Japanese fishing licences. Yonemura said some whites wanted to stop all the Japanese fishing. Mankichi did not believe him. He had lived and fought with the white people, and when he told the Japanese fishermen not to worry, they believed him.

In August, 1922, the commission visited Port Essington. The Japanese were ready to present their case. But only the white and native Indian fishermen were called to appear before the

*Repairing gill nets after a week of fishing.*

commission. The commission had twelve meetings in different places, but not one Japanese was invited.

Yonemura said, "There are six members on the commission. Four are members of Parliament from the salmon-fishing areas. They don't want to hear from us because we do not have the vote." Mankichi could not believe this. Most of the Japanese had taken out Canadian citizenship. Surely their living would not be taken away.

In the following spring, the cannery manager called the Japanese fishermen together. He looked unhappy. "I have bad news," he said. "Japanese fishing licences are to be cut by 40 per cent. It means 120 of you will no longer be able to fish at Port Essington."

There were angry speeches but it was futile. Some of the men sneered at Mankichi: "That's the kind of government you fought for!" They decided that the single men would lose their licences, and a special fund was raised to help them. But this was only the beginning. In 1925, the government ordered another 15 per cent cut, and 28 men lost their licences. The men with the least number of years volunteered to be cut. In the following two years 30 more licences were lost. Men able to find other work went south. There was great fear in the Japanese fishing community.

The fishermen hired a lawyer to present their case to the Supreme Court of Canada. For the first time in many years there was rejoicing amongst the Japanese in Port Essington. The court ruled that the cuts were unlawful. Any British subject had the right to receive a fishing licence. The government appealed the case to the Privy Council in London, England. The Privy Council agreed with the Supreme Court of Canada – to deny a licence because of a man's origin was unlawful. It was discrimination.

But in 1929 the Government of Canada passed a new law. The Minister of Fisheries was given the right to deny licences to anyone. The Japanese were bewildered. There seemed to be no justice.

Mankichi grew bitter and angry. As the towboat pulled the Japanese crafts down the river, he watched the white and Indian fishermen go by in their boats powered by gas engines. Japanese fishermen were not allowed to use engines! The more he thought of it, the angrier he became. The next week he had a gas engine placed in his boat. Yonemura begged him not to do it. "They will take away your licence," he said.

It had to happen. Mankichi watched the fishing patrol boat approach as he went down the river, the gas engine *put-putting* loudly. He saw Stan Polesena, the Fisheries Officer who had also served in the 50th Battalion, watching him through his binoculars. He waved to Mankichi; the fishing patrol boat turned abruptly and headed away. Mankichi had mixed feelings.

A final protest was made by the Japanese fishermen in 1931. This time they were supported by white fishermen, cannery owners and other citizens. They all said the same thing – that the treatment of the Japanese fishermen was unnecessary, unjust, inhuman, and unwise. The government made no further moves against the Japanese. In the ten years between 1921 and 1931, 935 Japanese fishermen had lost their licences.

In the same year, 1931, Mankichi and the other Japanese veterans finally got the right to vote.

1. You are representing one of these groups before the government commission: the native Indian fishermen; the white fishermen; the Japanese Canadian fishermen. Present an argument to show why you think members of your group should be given licences to fish for salmon.
2. Use your dictionary and look up the meaning of the word *discrimination*. In what ways did the government discriminate against the Japanese Canadians before 1931?

Right: *A cannery wharf at a British Columbia fishing settlement. The gill nets were placed in the tanks for cleaning after a week of fishing. The fishermen lived on the first floor of the buildings. The nets were stored on the second floor. Notice the rollers used to pull the nets up to the net lofts for storage.*

# The Second Generation: Kenji and Chiyo Omura

## GROWING UP IN PORT ESSINGTON

**Japanese expressions**

When Kenji and Chiyo left for school or went out to play, they called out *itte mairi masu,* which means "I am going." Oya replied *itte irrashai,* "Be on your way." When they returned home they said *tadaima,* "I have arrived."

This custom went back to the days when Japan was troubled by constant warfare between different groups. It was dangerous for anyone to leave the safety of the home. Whenever a person had to go on an errand, he announced *itte mairi masu.* Then the family gathered at the entrance of the house, bowed and said *itte irrashai.* These expressions were prayers for the safety of the person who was leaving.

At the beginning of a meal, Kenji and Chiyo were taught to say *itadaki masu,* which translated means "I accept the meal." This is a form of grace. At the end of the meal they said *gochiso sama,* which means "I have enjoyed the meal."

In 1922 a son was born to Mankichi and Oya Omura. They called him Kenji. He was born in the middle of the sockeye season. It was a good time for a baby to arrive. In Port Essington the hospital was open only during the summer. Mankichi heard the good news from the collector boat and came home early on Friday afternoon. He knew Oya would not want him to return home in the middle of the week, as the sockeye season was too short to interrupt. Chiyo, a sister for Kenji, was born in 1925.

*Port Essington Public School, grades 4 to 8, in the 1930s.*

When Kenji started school he spoke and understood only Japanese. His teacher at the one-room school was Mr. William Jones. There were more Japanese than white children in the school. All the Japanese children spoke their language freely. Even the white children were able to understand many Japanese phrases. Mr Jones did not like this.

After the regular school day the Japanese children attended the Japanese school. Here they learned to read and write Japanese. Mankichi and Oya wanted their children to learn about Japan and Japanese customs. But in the Japanese school, the Nisei (pronounced nee-say, meaning "second generation") children chatted in English. This annoyed Mr. Shinkuro Kozai, the Japanese teacher, who had difficulty in understanding English.

Mr. Jones and Mr. Kozai got together one day and made an agreement. Only English was to be used in the Port Essington school and only Japanese in the Japanese language school. They agreed to be strict about this rule. The plan was a success. From Mr. Jones the Nisei children learned to speak, read, and write English. They also learned British and Canadian history. Mankichi and Oya felt that the two children received a good education from Mr. Jones, who made them work hard. At the end of the grade eight year, high-school entrance examinations had to be taken. Mr. Jones' pupils had a good record.

In the Japanese language school Kenji and Chiyo learned that Japanese books started from what is the back of an English book. The printing went vertically from the top to the bottom of the page, and from right to left. They first learned to read *katakana*, which was a printed Japanese alphabet. Then they learned *hiragana*, which was the alphabet written in a script form. Picture words were introduced gradually. This involved much memory work and the children had to work hard. Often they wished they could go out to play with their white and Indian friends.

At the end of the lesson the boys and girls were required to sweep the room, clean the blackboard and wipe the desks with a wet rag. Two pupils did this every day. This is the custom in Japanese schools.

## Playing Jan-Ken-Po

Jan-ken-po is a very popular game with Japanese children. The game can be played by two people or by two groups.

The players face each other. They say together "Jan-ken-po"; at "po" all throw out their right hands, showing either

a clenched fist meaning a *stone*

or an open hand meaning *paper*

or two fingers meaning *scissors*

The rules are :

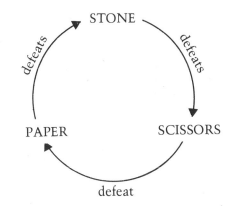

If playing as a team, the players need a short meeting to decide what to do.

The first to win five times is the winner of the game.

Instead of tossing a coin, play jan-ken-po!

# Learn Some Japanese

This is *hiragana*, the Japanese alphabet in script form that Kenji and Chiyo learned to read in school. The chart follows the pattern for reading *hiragana*.

Remember that you read from the top to the bottom of the page and from right to left. When you reach the bottom of one column in the chart, move to the top of the next one.

| | | | | | | CONSONANTS | | | | | START HERE ↓ |
|---|---|---|---|---|---|---|---|---|---|---|---|
| | W | R | Y | M | H | N | T | S | K | VOWELS |
| ん OON | わ WA | ら RA | や YA | ま MA | は HA | な NA | た TA | さ SA | か KA | あ A |
| | | り RI | | み MI | ひ HI | に NI | ち CHI | し SHI | き KI | い I |
| | | る RU | ゆ YU | む MU | ふ FU | ぬ NU | つ TSU | す SU | く KU | う U |
| | | れ RE | | め ME | へ HE | ね NE | て TE | せ SE | け KE | え E |
| | を O | ろ RO | よ YO | も MO | ほ HO | の NO | と TO | そ SO | こ KO | お O |

Japanese vowels are pronounced differently from English vowels. Here is a guide that will help you to read the *hiragana* chart:

a  ah    e  eh
i  ee    o  oh
u  oo

Can you pronounce these Japanese words? For example, the word for 'star' is pronounced *ho-shi*. Use the *hiragana* chart for reference.

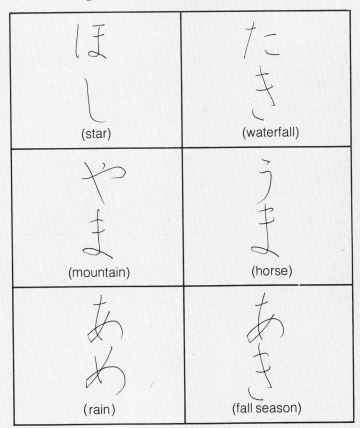

(star)

(waterfall)

(mountain)

(horse)

(rain)

(fall season)

Can you write these words in *hiragana?* Remember that you write from top to bottom, not left to right. Use the *hiragana* chart for reference.

1. ne-ko (cat)
2. i-nu (dog)
3. sa-to (sugar)
4. i-shi (stone)
5. ma-chi (village)
6. fu-ne (ship)
7. mo-mo (peach)
8. ka-sa (umbrella)
9. ha-ma (beach)
10. u-shi (cow)

Japanese picture words are called *characters.* They were borrowed from Chinese writing. Children finishing elementary school in Japan are able to read about 880 characters. A high school graduate knows about 1850 characters.

Can you see the pattern in the characters below?

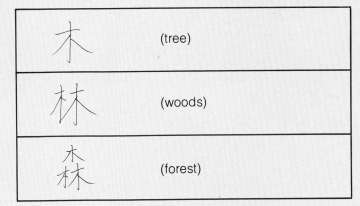

木 (tree)

林 (woods)

森 (forest)

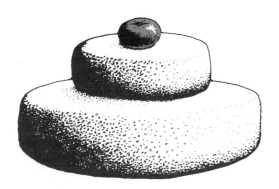

Kagami mochi

Japanese Canadians in the 1970s celebrate the New Year by pounding rice to make kagami mochi.

Opposite page: *A concert in Vancouver. The signs in Japanese script tell how much money people attending the concert gave towards expenses.*

## SPECIAL DAYS AT PORT ESSINGTON

### The New Year

The biggest holiday of the year for the Japanese Canadians was New Year's Day. The week before January 1, the Omuras and their neighbours gathered together and held a *mochi tsuki*, the making of rice cakes. Steamed rice was placed in a container and pounded with a big wooden mallet. The loud pounding could be heard over most of Port Essington. The men handled the mallet and the women shifted the rice and added water to prevent it from sticking. This was done between each stroke of the mallet, and the women had to be very alert. Two large round cakes of white *mochi* were used to make a *kagami mochi*. The smaller cake was placed on the larger one and usually topped with a Japanese orange. The *kagami mochi* was placed on a shelf as a symbol of happiness.

Another custom was to place a pine tree outside near the front door. This was called *kado matsu*. Kenji used to go with his father to the woods to cut down the tree. The pine tree, because it is strong and always green, signifies strength and long life. Noodles, which stand for long life, were always served on New Year's Eve. On the last day of the year, Oya scrubbed the house from top to bottom.

On New Year's Day new clothes were ready for Kenji and Chiyo. They greeted their parents, saying *Shin nen omedeto*, which means "Happy New Year." Oya served *ozoni*, a special soup that contains small toasted square *mochi*. In keeping with tradition, each person ate one *mochi* for each year of life.

Mankichi, as the head of the family, visited their neighbours and friends. He wished them *Shin nen omedeto*. He thanked them for their kindness over the past year. Toasts were made with *sake* and special food served. Oya, at home, received the guests who called at the Omura home. Some were white and Indian friends.

### Concerts

Another highlight of the year for the Japanese Canadians and for Port Essington was the concert held once a year. This attracted people from other fishing settlements too. There was no charge for admission, but families gave a donation as they came in. Everyone

knew how much each family gave. A slip of paper with the amount written on it was hung from a long rope strung from the back to the front of the hall.

The program was usually quite long, and families brought refreshments. The Japanese Young Men's Society presented plays about old Japan. It was exciting for Kenji and Chiyo to watch the curtain open with a series of jerks accompanied by the slow loud banging of the wooden clappers. Everyone knew the stories, and the audience gave loud cries of approval and encouragement when the actors did a scene well.

Mr. Yonemura would perform *naniwabushi*, a mixture of singing and storytelling with music. He played the *shamisen*, a string instrument something like a guitar, for accompaniment. The audience often joined in.

## Dominion Day

Dominion Day, July 1, was a big day for the Indian people of the area. They gathered at Port Essington for a program of boat races and tug of war. In the baseball games Japanese, Indians and whites joined together to form a community team. The Port Essington team was always one of the strongest.

## The O-Bon Festival

The O-Bon festival is celebrated by the Japanese to remember the people who have died. In Port Essington it was held in August. The entire Japanese community visited the cemetery just beyond the Indian reservation. Kenji and Chiyo helped tidy the graves. Offerings of food were left at each grave and incense burned. The Buddhist priest conducted a service in the cemetery.

The O-Bon festival is a happy occasion, and at Port Essington a dance, the *O-Bon odori*, was held in the evening. Japanese kimonos made a colourful sight as the dancers went through simple but graceful steps in a large circle.

*Houses of the Indian reservation, Port Essington, 1910.*

*Looking north across the Skeena River from Port Essington, 1915. At the right is a cannery; at the left is a wharf. Locate these features on the map of Port Essington.*

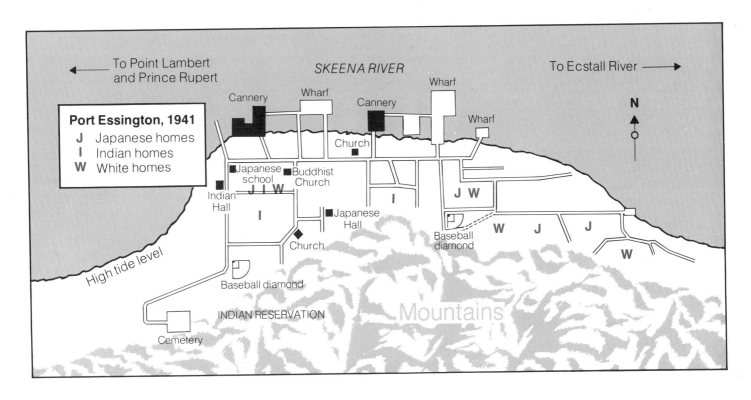

**Port Essington, 1941**
J   Japanese homes
I   Indian homes
W   White homes

To Point Lambert and Prince Rupert ←

SKEENA RIVER

To Ecstall River →

Cannery

Wharf

Cannery

Wharf

Wharf

Church

N

Japanese school

Buddhist Church

J  I  W

Indian Hall

I

J  W

I

Japanese Hall

J  W

Church

W  J  J

Baseball diamond

W

High tide level

Baseball diamond

INDIAN RESERVATION

Mountains

Cemetery

Port Essington had a population of about 300 when Kenji was growing up. It is now a deserted town. The three canneries closed down one by one as the fishing boundary was moved downstream. A fire in July, 1961, destroyed many of the buildings.

1. What information on the map shows that the people made their living from the sea?
2. Look at the housing pattern in Port Essington. What evidence is there that the different nationalities in the community lived side by side?
3. What other information have you read that shows that Indian, white and Japanese people lived side by side?
4. Discuss the advantages of living in a community like Port Essington with Indian, white and Japanese people.

# ATTENDING HIGH SCHOOL

It was a happy day for the Omura family when Kenji passed his high-school entrance examination. Mankichi and Oya visited Mr. Jones and presented him with a small gift of appreciation. It is usual for the Japanese to give gifts to celebrate important events, such as the building of a new home, or someone taking a long trip. When people visit the homes of their friends and neighbours, they take a small gift, an *omiyage,* such as candies or fruit. The custom requires that a gift be given in return.

There was no high school in Port Essington. Mankichi and Oya decided that Kenji should attend a technical high school in Vancouver. The day before Kenji left, Oya prepared a special dinner with *sekihan,* red rice, to mark the occasion. Mr. Yonemura and other neighbours gave Kenji an envelope with money. A going-away gift such as this is called *senbetsu.* Mr. Jones came to wish him good luck and gave Kenji a pen. Mankichi and Oya were most appreciative of Mr. Jones' gift, and sent him a basket of vegetables from the family garden.

Many friends and neighbours came to the wharf to say goodbye. Kenji stood on the deck of the *Cardena* for a long time as it left Port Essington. He watched the gill-netters fishing for cohoe. The boats from the different canneries were identified by the flags painted on their sides. The Claxton cannery flag was similar to the flag of Japan – a red ball on a white background. No wonder, he thought, some white people claimed the Skeena River was invaded by spy ships of the Japanese navy.

In Vancouver Kenji boarded in a rooming house on Powell Street. He enrolled in the Vancouver Technical School and in the Japanese Language School on Alexander Street. After each regular school day Kenji, with about 1000 other pupils, spent one and a half hours learning to speak and write Japanese at the Language School. The principal was Mr. Tsutae Sato. He often told the children that learning the Japanese language would help them become better Canadians. "Learning about Japan and its people will enable you to help other Canadians better understand Japan. You will be a bridge for understanding," he said.

Opposite page: *A class at the Japanese Language School on Alexander Street in Vancouver. The teacher (centre) is Mr. Sato.*

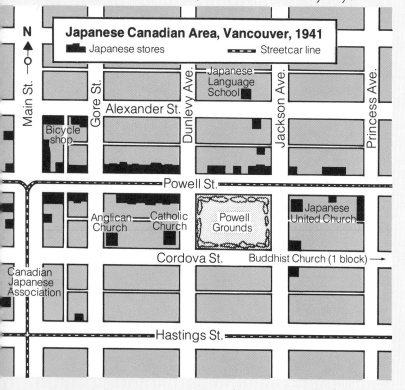

# The Powell Street Community

Powell Street was the centre of the Japanese community in Vancouver. There were many small stores that sold almost everything the Japanese needed. There were grocery stores, tailor and barber shops, restaurants and dry-cleaning stores. Japanese foodstuffs were manufactured in small shops and sold in the grocery stores. The businesses were organized into associations by the Japanese. Above many of the stores were the rooming houses that were homes to the single men in the early days.

By the 1930s the community also had a Catholic Church, an Anglican Church, a United Church and a Buddhist Church. Most of the Japanese were Buddhists. The Buddhist ministers were trained in Japan. In the Sunday schools the children were taught the customs and traditions of Japan. All the services were in Japanese. In the Christian churches, services were in English and Japanese. The ministers were trained in Canada. The Nisei often visited churches of other Canadians. These exchange visits were one time when the Japanese met other Canadians.

The Japanese Language School on Alexander Street was started in 1909. As the Japanese realized that they would not be returning to Japan, their children began to attend regular public schools to learn English. After school hours, they went to the Japanese Language School. This school also served as a community centre. Movies, meetings, and concerts took place in the school auditorium.

Of the 23 000 Japanese people in Canada in 1942, about 8000 lived in or near the Powell Street area. Almost all the remainder lived in other parts of British Columbia – in the Fraser Valley, the Okanagan Valley, on Vancouver Island, or in fishing villages along the coast. Only a small number lived east of the Rocky Mountains.

1. Locate the areas shown in the photographs on the map of Powell Street area.
2. What clues in the photographs show that the pictures were taken in an area where Japanese Canadians lived?
3. Suggest reasons why the Japanese Canadians lived together in one area in Vancouver.
4. What do you think were the disadvantages of this arrangement for the Japanese? What may have been the advantages?

*The corner of Main and Powell looking east along Powell Street, 1938.*

*Bicycle shop on Main Street, north of Powell.*

A Japanese Canadian delegation went to Ottawa in 1936, seeking the right to vote. Members were (left to right) Samuel Hayakawa, Minoru Kobayashi, Hide Hyodo and Dr. E. Banno.

Life in Vancouver was very different from life in a small fishing community on the Skeena River. There were tall buildings, streetcars, movie theatres, libraries, department stores, radio stations and three daily newspapers.

The newspapers often had articles that criticized the Japanese community. They said the schools did not help the Nisei become good Canadian citizens. But Kenji was glad he was able to write letters that his parents could read. He was pleased to learn even a little about the country from which his parents had come. The newspapers also said the Japanese did not want to live like the white people, that they were happy to live in poorer homes and eat only rice and fish. But Kenji knew that many Japanese wished they could buy better homes. They certainly enjoyed good food as much as anyone. It was difficult for the Japanese. They had the lowest paying jobs, usually with hard physical work. When they worked alongside the whites, they were paid less for the same work. This always made them dissatisfied. The whites also said the Japanese took jobs that belonged to "real" Canadians. They were not allowed to vote in elections at any level. The newspapers reported that the Japanese could not be assimilated into Canadian life. Kenji did not know exactly what this meant, but he knew he was different from his parents.

In the city he saw motion pictures, read books, magazines and newspapers, and listened to the radio. His parents did not do any of these things because they did not understand English well enough. Each summer when he returned to the Skeena he wished he could talk about these things with his parents, but he did not feel his knowledge of Japanese was good enough.

Kenji often heard the older people complaining about the Nisei. They said that the Nisei had no respect for their elders, lacked good manners, didn't work hard enough, and had no pioneer spirit. In the 1930s, when the Nisei began to leave school they organized the Japanese Canadian Citizens' League, and published a newspaper in English, called *The New Canadian*. Through these two channels they presented the viewpoint of Japanese people, many of whom had taken out Canadian citizenship or were Canadian born. In 1936 the Nisei decided to send a delegation to Ottawa to try to get the right to vote. They were not successful. Many older Japanese said the Nisei were *namaiki,* meaning impertinent and cheeky, to do such a thing.

Kenji concluded that the older folk were complaining because the Nisei were becoming too Canadian. At the same time, the white people were complaining that the Japanese were not Canadian enough.

## AFTER HIGH SCHOOL GRADUATION

Kenji graduated from high school in 1940. He was the top student in his drafting class. He visited many companies and wrote many letters, but could not find a job. Canadian companies did not hire Japanese Canadians. Even Nisei university graduates went to work in pulp and paper mills and in logging camps as labourers. A number of Nisei gave up and went to Japan, only to find they were out of place there as well.

War had broken out in Europe in 1939, but Japanese Canadians were rejected by the Canadian Army. Then all Japanese Canadians were ordered to register with the Royal Canadian Mounted Police. Each person was required to carry a card at all times. The card had the person's name, address, age, height, weight, occupation, photograph, thumb print, and a number.

Kenji felt discouraged and depressed. He had a sad feeling that he was an outsider and not a part of his own country. He returned to the Skeena to work as a fisherman.

## THE LONG TRIP SOUTH

On December 7, 1941, Kenji heard on the radio that Japanese planes had attacked the United States' naval base at Pearl Harbour in the Hawaiian Islands. Japan and the United States were at war. Canada declared war on Japan. That evening all windows had to be covered. There was to be a complete blackout along the coast in case of a Japanese attack.

One week later Kenji was cutting firewood when he saw the R.C.M.P. constable approaching the house. This was strange, since

1. What government actions helped make Japanese Canadians feel like "second-class" citizens before 1940?
2. Give examples of the arguments white people probably used to back their claim that Japanese Canadians were not "Canadian enough."
3. How would you have answered these arguments if you had been a Nisei?

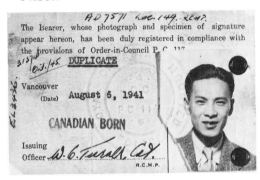

*Even before Canada declared war on Japan in December, 1941, all Japanese Canadians were ordered to carry identity cards.*

the Mountie was stationed at Port Essington only during the summer. He told Kenji that all Japanese Canadian boats still in the water had to go to Inverness Cannery. At the Cannery, Kenji was ordered to go to Tusk's Inlet near Prince Rupert. There he found other Japanese Canadian gill-netters anchored. A navy corvette stood by.

Kenji was not allowed to go home and had to live on board. He managed to get some food from his friends, but the boat was very cold as it was not equipped for winter. Two days later sailors from the corvette told the fishermen to take their boats to Vancouver. The men complained that they were not equipped for a trip of 800 kilometres in the middle of winter. Their families would not know what had happened to them. Two men were allowed to go to Prince Rupert and returned with food that they purchased on credit. It was enough for two days. They brought back coal, but only one fourth of the boats had stoves.

On December 16 at 8.30 A.M. they started out. Two seiners, which were larger fishing boats, towed a long line of 30 gill-netters. They were escorted by a corvette and tugboat. Two days later they entered Milbanke Sound and the waters became rough. Twice the line broke and the corvette crew spent three hours repairing the damage. Kenji was cold and wet to the bone. He was stiff from bracing himself against the waves that pounded the small boat. The cold sea water constantly sprayed over into the cabin. Near Bella Bella they ran into log strewn waters and one boat smashed its bow badly. On Christmas Day they reached Alert Bay. Kenji went to the fishing village, sent a wire to his parents and bought a chicken. With boiled cabbage it was Christmas dinner.

Fifteen days after leaving Tusk's Inlet they reached Steveston at the mouth of the Fraser River. The Japanese fishermen there took them in, gave them a place to sleep and money to get home.

When Kenji saw his father's boat for the last time tied up at the mouth of the Fraser, the deck rails were broken, the tie post was lost, and a deep gash on the right side marked where it had slammed into another boat. It was later sold by the government for a small sum of money, which was sent to Mankichi.

Right: *In 1941, hundreds of fishing boats taken from Japanese Canadians were gathered at New Westminster. Seven weeks later they were sold by the government.*

1. Suggest reasons why the Canadian government distrusted Japanese Canadians in 1941.
2. Suggest reasons why the Japanese Canadian fishing boats were rounded up.
3. Discuss whether a government should be able to take a person's property and sell it without the owner's consent.

In Vancouver, Kenji stayed with a friend on Powell Street. The government had closed the Japanese Language School and stopped the publication of the three Japanese newspapers. Only *The New Canadian*, the Nisei paper published in English, was allowed to continue. All cars, radios, and cameras were confiscated. Many people lost their jobs. Angry letters appeared in the Canadian newspapers when Canadian soldiers were killed in the Battle of Hong Kong. The letters blamed the Japanese Canadians and said they should be put in detention camps. Rumours filled the Japanese community.

Twenty-five days after Kenji had seen the R.C.M.P. constable approach him, he returned home in the same clothes he had worn when he was cutting firewood.

*A Japanese Canadian turns over his car to a police officer. Cameras and radios were also confiscated.*

# Sumi-e

The word *sumi-e* translated means "ink picture." Traditionally ink paintings in Japan were on rice paper or silk. Only one colour, black, was used. Modern artists still use the traditional black but are free to add other colours.

In the photograph, Mary Nakamura is painting a *sumi-e* on rice paper. To make her ink she filled the special ink stone at the left with water and rubbed it with an ink stick. One basic stroke for the artist to master is a side stroke of the brush made with the arm moving free in the air above the paper, as shown in the photograph.

# EVACUATION

In March 1942, the R.C.M.P. constable came to Port Essington again. All Japanese Canadian families were ordered to leave their homes in one week. When Kenji explained to Oya that the government felt the Japanese Canadians might cause trouble and help the Japanese army, she found this difficult to understand.

Each person was allowed to take two suitcases. Many prized family belongings had to be left behind. Slowly the Japanese Canadians gathered at the cannery wharf. Their white and Indian friends came down to see them off. There were tears and sad goodbyes.

The Japanese Canadian people boarded a scow that was pulled across the river by a boat. Henry Reed operated the boat and tried to make it as easy as possible. But one veteran angrily threw his medals in the water. "We are herded like cattle," he exclaimed. Across the Skeena River at Haysport, a train filled with other Japanese Canadian fishermen and their families waited for them.

Escorted by R.C.M.P. constables the train took three days to reach Vancouver. There the train pulled into Hastings Park, at the Exhibition grounds. The Skeena group of evacuees was the first to arrive. Kenji and the others were put to work cleaning the buildings and making bunk beds. Men and women were separated. Chiyo worked in the kitchen. No one was allowed to leave the Park, and everyone had to be inside from sunset to sunrise. Their letters were examined by a censor, an official whose job was to make sure the letters were not helping the enemy.

Then the government announced that all Japanese Canadians were to be moved away from the coast. They started with the men. Some Nisei refused to cooperate unless families were kept together. The government imprisoned them in camps with German prisoners-of-war in northern Ontario. Later the government changed its mind and began to move families as groups.

After a two-month stay in Hastings Park, the Omura family was sent to Sandon in the Kootenay Valley. Sandon was a ghost town, an old mining centre that had been abandoned years before. Kenji once

Left: *These orders appeared in* The New Canadian, *April 29, 1942.*

*Unloading possessions in Alberta. Japanese Canadians were sent to work on sugar-beet farms in Alberta and Manitoba.*

again found himself cleaning old buildings and making repairs. When that was completed, he and other young men were sent to New Denver on the shores of Slocan Lake to build three-room cabins in an old orchard.

By September 1942, 21 439 Japanese had been evacuated from the British Columbia coast. Over half were in places like Sandon and New Denver. Others went to sugar-beet farms in Alberta, Manitoba, and Ontario. Seven hundred were in detention camps. Most of them were Canadian citizens and had committed no crimes.

1. In times of crisis the Canadian government can enforce the War Measures Act, which gives it wide powers. This Act made it legal for the authorities to move the Japanese Canadians. Discuss whether you think it is right for the government to have these powers in time of war.

---

# FOR SALE BY TENDER

## Corner Grocery Store
### Main and Powell Streets

The Authorized Deputy of the Secretary of State of Canada and /or the Custodian, offers for sale by tender the Grocery business at 191 Main Street, formerly operated by Tomijiro NAKA.

The store will be open for inspection of the stock, etc. on the seventeenth and eighteenth days of November, between the hours of one p.m. and five p.m.

---

*During the war the government sold the Japanese Canadian homes and businesses, although at the time of evacuation the people were told they would keep their properties.*

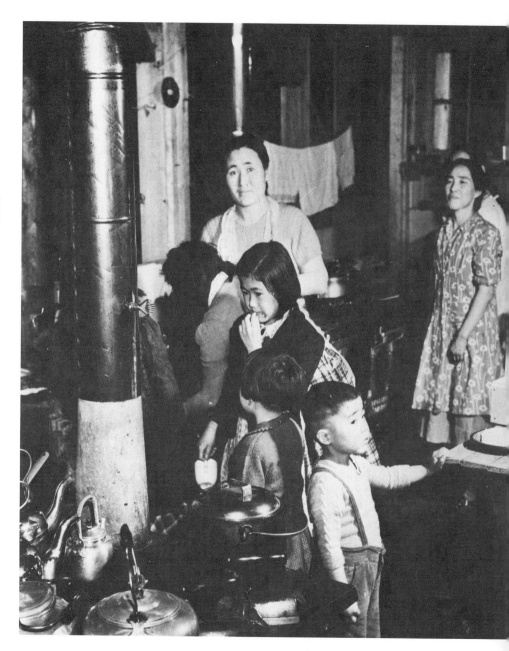

*A community kitchen in an interior town. Two families shared each three-room cabin and cooked on one stove. The cabins were cold and drafty in winter.*

# ON ACTIVE SERVICE

In 1944 Kenji read in *The New Canadian* that the Canadian government was recruiting Japanese Canadians in Ontario. The British Army needed men who could speak Japanese for service in Burma. Kenji told his parents that he wanted to enlist. Mankichi and Oya were not happy. But they went with Mr. Yonemura to New Denver to see him off.

With 30 other Nisei, Kenji swore allegiance to the King and enlisted in the Canadian Army at the Toronto Exhibition grounds. They were all sent to No. 20 Basic Infantry Training Camp at Brantford, Ontario. The Nisei were kept together as a platoon in B Company. They trained hard and they learned fast.

From Brantford Kenji went to Vancouver to attend the Canadian Army Japanese Language School. Kenji and the five other Nisei with him were able to graduate from a 12-month course at the Language School in eight weeks, because of their previous training. They were promoted to the rank of sergeant, and went overseas as members of the Canadian Intelligence Corps.

By the time Kenji and his group reached the British Intelligence Corps depot in India, the war was over. But they were needed for clean-up work. Kenji flew to Singapore to assist in the program of returning Japanese soldiers to their homeland. From there he was posted to Hong Kong for 14 months.

In Hong Kong he worked with the men investigating war crimes against Canadian soldiers who had fought in the Battle of Hong Kong. With Major J. B. Puddicombe, the Canadian prosecutor, he tramped the hills of Hong Kong Island to determine how the battle had been fought. On some of his lone walks he saw the graves of the Canadian soldiers. It was ironic, Kenji thought, that the first Canadian to visit these graves was a Japanese Canadian. In 1947, Sergeant Kenji Omura returned to Canada.

A Bill was passed in the legislature of British Columbia on March 7, 1949. It gave all Japanese Canadians the right to vote. On April 1, 1949, all restrictions on Japanese Canadian citizens were lifted.

*Overseas service in World War II. Sergeant Roy Ito with Major-General Tanaka (right) who commanded a Japanese regiment at the Battle of Hong Kong. The Canadian sergeant was going over the battle area where many Canadians died in 1941. About 150 Nisei served in the army.*

# The Third Generation:
# Robert and Mary Omura

## A NEW LIFE

After he left the army, Kenji decided to live in Toronto. He asked his parents to join him, but they stayed in New Denver. They felt they were too old to start a new life or to go back to the Skeena.

Kenji had no difficulty finding work as a draftsman. Japanese Canadians were now able to get jobs in nearly every line of work. Some were engineers, doctors, lawyers, teachers, nurses and architects. Many worked in government departments and in factories. The change from the pre-war days in British Columbia was remarkable. Some Nisei said the forced movement had been a good thing. Others could not agree.

There were almost 11 000 Japanese Canadians living in Toronto, but they were scattered all over the city. There were a few Japanese groceries and restaurants, but nothing that could be compared to Powell Street in Vancouver before the war. Many Japanese Canadians returned to Vancouver, but they too were scattered all over the city.

Kenji married a Nisei girl, Sadako Kodama, and they bought a home. A son, Robert, was born. Sadako joined the Home and School Association when their son started school. She became secretary of the association. Then a daughter, Mary, was born. As the two children grew up, they took part in the same activities as other children in their neighbourhood. Robert joined the Cubs; Mary became a Brownie. They took piano lessons. Robert joined the hockey team.

Only when the children went to the Buddhist Church did they see other Japanese Canadians and Sansei (pronounced san-say, meaning "third generation") children. In the Buddhist Church the service was completely in English. A Japanese Language School was started in Toronto, but Robert and Mary did not go. They said it was

*A 1970 photograph of Nisei parents, Mr. and Mrs. Roy Ito, with their Sansei children.*

1. How did the forced movement of the Japanese Canadians change the community?
2. Why did some Japanese Canadians think the forced movement was a "good thing"? Why did others disagree?
3. Discuss these statements:

   Children should have to learn the language of their grandparents.

   Children should not have to learn the language of their grandparents.

too far to travel and they were not interested. They did not understand any Japanese and English was always spoken in their home. Japanese customs were all but forgotten, although their family enjoyed Japanese food.

Robert and Mary often heard their parents talking about Vancouver and about the evacuation. It was hard for them to believe such things had happened.

In July, 1960, Kenji and Sadako sat the children down and read them a news item. The Bill of Rights had been passed in the House of Commons with every member of Parliament voting in favour of the Bill. From then on, every Canadian, regardless of race, nationality, colour, religion or sex would enjoy the following rights: the right to enjoy private property; the right to be tried in a court of law if accused of a crime; the right to freedom of religion; the right to freedom of speech; the right to freedom of assembly and association; and the right to freedom of the press. Japanese Canadians, Kenji and Sadako told their children, had lost all these rights except one during World War II. In passing the Bill, members of Parliament had said the experience of the Japanese Canadians was one reason why it was needed.

55

# Japanese Canadians Today

## THE JAPANESE CANADIAN CULTURAL CENTRE

In June, 1964, the Japanese Canadian Cultural Centre in Toronto was opened by Prime Minister Lester B. Pearson. It was built to honour the first Japanese immigrants to Canada. One of the aims of the Centre is to make other Canadians aware of aspects of Japanese culture. Several of the programs that are held are illustrated here.

*Mrs. Katsu Morino demonstrates* shodo, *the art of writing Japanese using a brush. The black ink used in* shodo *is similar to the ink used for* sumi-e – *the ink stone and the ink stick can be seen in the box at the left. The two basic brush strokes are also used in* sumi-e.

*Vivian Yatabe practises* origami, *the Japanese art of paper folding. If you are interested in learning how to make some of these colourful decorations, the bibliography on page 64 lists some books about* origami.

Top left: *The Japanese Canadian Cultural Centre in Toronto, designed by Raymond Moriyama.*

Top right: *Classes are held in* kendo, *Japanese fencing with bamboo swords.*

Left: *Classes in judo at the Centre are popular with young people.*
*It is the ambition of many learners to reach the highest level and earn a black belt.*

Left: *Bonsai, the art of growing dwarf potted plants, is an ancient practice in Japan. The art is based on skilful pruning of roots and branches, and painstaking training of the plant. Classes in bonsai are held at the Centre.*

*Doll-making is a highly developed craft in Japan. The warrior (*right*), the fisherman (*lower right*), and the girl (*below*) are all handmade.*

# CONTRIBUTIONS OF SOME JAPANESE CANADIANS

*George Tanaka, landscape artist. Mr. Tanaka designed the centennial gardens in Stratford, Ontario, and in Mississauga, Ontario.*

*Raymond Moriyama, architect. In addition to the Japanese Canadian Cultural Centre, Mr. Moriyama designed the Ontario Science Centre, the Scarborough Civic Centre, the London Art Gallery, and the Toronto Public Library.*

60

*Tom Shoyama, economist. Editor of* The New Canadian, *1939-1945. Deputy Minister of Finance, 1975.*

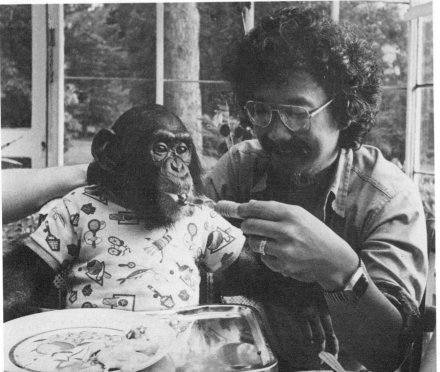

Top left: *Irene Uchida, Professor, McMaster University Medical Centre. During International Women's-Year, Dr. Uchida was recognized by the Ontario Government as one of the 25 outstanding women of the province for her work in medical science.*

Lower left: *David Suzuki, Professor of Zoology at the University of British Columbia. Dr. Suzuki is a host of many CBC science programs.*

61

# Ikebana, the Art of Flower Arranging

The word *ikebana* is translated as "flower arrangement," but the real meaning to the Japanese people is not expressed by this translation. Ikebana is the art of placing carefully selected flowers in a container so as to reveal their true nature.

The arranger has to follow basic rules that have been laid down as the art has developed over hundreds of years. The container and the flowers are very carefully chosen. Traditionally, there are three main points of focus in the arrangement – heaven, earth and man. Together these represent the universe. In this way, the flower arrangement has a spiritual meaning and is meant to show the harmony of man and nature.

## Nageire Arrangement

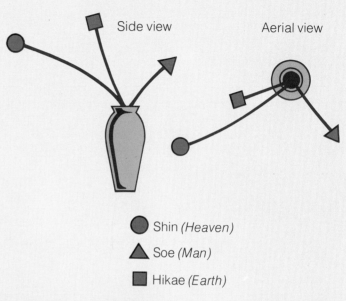

Side view       Aerial view

● Shin *(Heaven)*

▲ Soe *(Man)*

■ Hikae *(Earth)*

## Moribana Arrangement

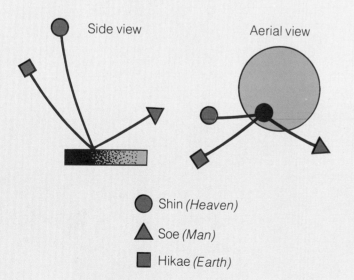

Side view       Aerial view

● Shin *(Heaven)*

▲ Soe *(Man)*

■ Hikae *(Earth)*

The diagrams illustrate two of the many styles of arrangement. *Nageire* means literally "thrown-in," and usually features one or two flowers arranged in as natural a way as possible in a simple container. There is a basic form in the arrangement. The length of each of the three main branches, heaven, earth and man, is determined by the size of the container. In the arrangement illustrated, the measurement of the height and diameter of the container rim are added. The length of the *shin* or "heaven" stem is 1.5 times this measurement. *Moribana* means "piled-up flowers in a flat basin." A needle-point holder is used to keep the flowers in place. As with *nageire* there is a basic form underlying the length and placement of the main branches.

Below: *Mrs. Kiyoko Abe, who has spent years studying* ikebana, *works on a* moribana *arrangement.*

Right: *The finished arrangement.*

*In 1977 some 40 000 Japanese Canadians across Canada celebrated the Japanese Canadian Centennial. It was 100 years since Manzo Nagano, the first Japanese immigrant, arrived in Canada. The symbol of the Centennial, shown on Debbie Taniwa's T-shirt, was the Canadian maple leaf blended with the* sakura, *the Japanese cherry blossom.*

# FOR FURTHER STUDY

**Books**

Araki, Chiyoko. *Origami in the Classroom, Book 2* (M.G. Hurtig, Edmonton, 1968).

Cross, Kate. *Cooking Around the World* (Blandford, London, 1964). Includes some Japanese recipes.

Edmonds, I.G. *Case of the Marble Monster and Other Stories* (Scholastic Book Services, 1969). Folk tales of Japan.

Kogawa, Joy. *A Choice of Dreams* (McClelland and Stewart, 1974). Poems by a Japanese Canadian woman about her childhood.

Kunihiko, Kashari. *Creative Origami* (Japan Publications, Inc., Tokyo, 1967).

Patton, Janice. *The Exodus of the Japanese* (McClelland and Stewart, 1973). The story of the Japanese Canadians during World War II.

Tabrah, Ruth. *Momotaro: Peach Boy* (South Pacific Books, Rigby, 1973). A folk tale.

Takashima, Shizuye. *A Child in Prison Camp* (Tundra Books, 1971). The story of the author, a Japanese Canadian who was evacuated as a child from coastal British Columbia to the interior.

*Treasured Recipes,* Nisei Women's Club, Toronto. Available from the Japanese Canadian Cultural Centre, 123 Wynford Drive, Toronto.

**Audio-Visual**

*The Canadian Mosaic.* A series of eight sound filmstrips on different ethnic and racial groups and on cultural patterns in Canada. Available from Moreland-Latchford, 299 Queen Street West, Toronto.

*The Heart of Haiku,* Ann Atwood. (Lyceum Productions, 1971). Colour filmstrip and cassette.